Presented To

By

Listen, my son,
accept what I say,
and the years of
your life
will be many.

Proverbs 4:10
NIV

Listen my Son

Listen MY Son

THERE ARE plans FOR you!

AN INSPIRATIONAL GIFT BOOK

HOLLY DUNCAN

© 2015 Holly Duncan

LISTEN MY SON

Printed in the USA

Prepared for publication by: www.palmtreeproductions.com

ISBN (Print): 978-0-9965582-0-4
ISBN (Kindle): 978-0-9965582-1-1
ISBN (eBook): 978-0-9965582-2-8

Library of Congress Control Number: 2015910541

10 09 08 07 06   5 4 3 2 1

To Contact the Author:
WWW.HOLLYDUNCAN.COM

What Others Are Saying

There is great power in finding our identity in Christ. Many are searching for answers and for a defined purpose, wondering what life is truly about. In her book, *Listen My Son*, Holly Duncan challenges us to look not to ourselves for fulfillment and answers, but to look to the One who knows us and created us. She encourages us to be limitless and fearless dreamers.

Holly's words compel us to believe with the faith of a child— pure, unyielding, and genuine. *Listen My Son* invites us to dream with the Father, knowing that His strength in us can only propel us to greater things, all to glorify His name, all to further His Kingdom with an intentional love and purpose.

—Dr. Paul Tan
Senior Pastor, City Blessing Churches
Los Angeles, CA

Holly Duncan has not only taught me leadership, but also where its foundation lies and how the grandest visions are never impossible to achieve. She embodies the grace, zeal and altruism that every person should strive to have as they face challenges and journey through life.

Rusteen Haghi
Paul Merage School of Business
University of California

Holly Duncan's passion for seeing the purpose and destiny of young people fulfilled is her true calling in life. *Listen My Son* is focused on your role as a parent, grandparent, teacher, or mentor to train up these leaders of tomorrow and to help them understand the influence they can play in changing our culture. Through you they will learn they can influence society in a positive way!

DR. ED TUROSE
Executive Focus Coach
www.edturose.com

Holly Duncan inspires me. Yeah, she's my mom—but she loves the Lord and knows God has a plan for each one of us. She has taught me to talk to the Lord, listen, and step out in faith. She has encouraged me to find and follow my passion. I'm on my way to fulfilling my call ... and you can be, too!

JOSHUA DUNCAN
Holly's Son
Student, Azusa Pacific University

I wrote this book for all the mothers, grandmothers, teachers, and mentors who know the child you love has a bright, bold future that he is struggling to see for himself.

The words are meant for them, but they need to hear them spoken by you—filtered through your love, qualified by your desire for their highest good, and wrapped in how much you care.

These pages are meant to be a tool to help you connect with the one you love and find the words to help him discover how special he is, how important he is to God, and how simple it is to communicate with Him.

It is a big message delivered in just a few simple words. I pray you will find yourself delivering these words with courage and faith.

Listen
my Son

THERE ARE

plans

FOR you!

I hear you say to yourself,

"What am I going to do with my life?"

"Why am I here?"

"Why was I born?"

You are WONDERING about life ...

about *your* LIFE.

Let me assure you, you are not alone.

Many others—even your friends and peers—are wondering the same things.

They are asking the same questions.

But NO ONE talks about it ...

<u>no one</u>.

Don't FEAR.

Don't WORRY.

Don't FRET.

There are *plans* in store for *you!*

You have a WONDERFUL

future

ahead of **you**!

GOD, the Father of all things,

CREATOR of the universe,

created you in HIS image—

with an **_intentional_**

PURPOSE.

YOU KNIT ME
TOGETHER IN MY
MOTHER'S WOMB. I
PRAISE YOU BECAUSE
I AM FEARFULLY AND
WONDERFULLY MADE.

PSALMS 139:13-14
NIV

Listen my Son

You are not an ACCIDENT,

a SURPRISE,

a MISTAKE

or a MISFIT.

He created *you*.

You did not come from

pond scum (eww),

or descend from monkeys.

NO!

You had DIGNITY placed upon

you ... before you were ever created.

You are CROWNED with

dignity and **honor**.

See,

you are made

in the IMAGE

of

God.

Then God said, "Let us make mankind in our image, in our likeness," ... so God created mankind in His own image, in the image of God created He them: male and female He created them.

Genesis 1:25-27
NIV

Listen my Son

Wow!

That's amazing!

In God's IMAGE?

It's pretty hard to imagine, but that is what *He* says about *Us* in His WORD—the BIBLE.

God has even ordained what He wants YOU to **do** and **contribute** to this world.

Look at what He tells the prophet, Jeremiah:

Before I formed you
in the womb
I knew you ...

I set you apart;
I appointed you as
a prophet to the
nations.

Jeremiah 1:5
NIV

Listen my Son

God sent

specifically into the world.

Just like He did with

Jeremiah the prophet,

He **planned** something

specific for your LIFE.

The God of all creation has

PLANS for you!

Yes, you.

How exciting is that?

Who else would you want

planning your life?

He knows TODAY.

He knows TOMORROW.

He knows YOU intimately.

He knows the number of HAIRS
on your HEAD ... and that
changes every day!

(Matthew 10:29-31, Luke 12:6-17)

God cares ... He is deeply concerned about *every* area of your life.

He desires for you to live a life *full* of BLESSING.

Jesus came so *you*
could have *life*.

He came so you could
live your *life*

to the FULLEST!

(John 10:10)

There is NOTHING

you can't

talk to Him about.

NOTHING.

TALK.

That's all.

No big formula.

No ritual.

Just TALK.

TALK to HIM.

He CARES today.

He KNOWS.

He HOLDS the *future*.

The government doesn't
know the future.

The news media doesn't know.

Neither does your school ...

your parents ...

your boss ...

not even your friends.

Nobody knows the future except ...

... God.

God KNOWS.

Listen and *look* for
Him to LEAD YOU and
He will GUIDE YOU.
He is *faithful*.

He will do it!

He will encourage you and lead you

along the path to walk out your

destiny and *future*.

ONE STEP AT A TIME.

TALK, *listen*, STEP.

TALK, *listen*, STEP.

Without FEAR.

BE *confident.*

BE *bold.*

Listen my Son

God has given you gifts

and abilities for use in

the purpose for which

He has ordained you.

DEVELOP these gifts.

PRACTICE.

PLAY.

STUDY.

WORK.

TRAIN.

DEVELOP.

Grow.

For we are God's
handiwork,
created in Christ
Jesus to do
good works,
which God prepared
in advance
for us to do..

Ephesians 2:10
NIV

Listen my Son

Be a GOOD STEWARD

of those giftings.

Search for them

until you find out

what they are ... then

FIND WAYS TO USE THEM!

Be diligent.

Don't apologize for moving forward.

The *desires* in your heart

are GOD-GIVEN.

He put them there.

(Psalms 37:4)

These desires are like

buried treasures

for you to

DIG UP,

UNCOVER,

ENJOY,

and SHARE

with the world!

The dreams you have about what you want to accomplish, that crazy idea about who you see yourself becoming ... these came from God!

They are His way of pointing you in the right direction.

BELIEVE in *yourself*.

TRUST in *Him*.

No matter how far out of reach those dreams may feel, don't give up.

Take STEPS to achieve THEM.

STEP by STEP.

Keep STEPPING.

Others may not see it.

Keep STEPPING.

Walk

by

faith.

(2 Corinthians 5:7)

More will unfurl as you
continue to press forward.

Keep STEPPING.

You are on your way

to your SPHERE

—your *arena*—

the PURPOSE for which

you were *born*.

MAKE an *impact*.

LEAVE your **mark**.

Let your presence be

known and felt there.

Speak up.

Stand up.

Act.

Create.

Do.

Listen my Son

BRING *increase.*

BRING *change.*

BRING *reform*

to the world around you.

The world is waiting ...

FOR *you*.

Yes, **you**.

You've got some big things

to accomplish ...

... but you've got the

HELP

of a

big God!

A very BIG GOD indeed!

HOLLY DUNCAN

Holly Duncan cares about the next generation. They are her passion and the reason she is involved as the Student Leadership Director for Southlands Christian Schools. There she works with high school children, training them to lead and calling them to embrace and run hard after their destiny.

Married to Glenn for thirty years (March 2016), they have two grown children and a daughter-in-law. Together with her husband, she has served as an associate pastor to both youth and young adults as well as a leader in children's church. She is the Chapel Director of Southlands Christian Elementary School where she regularly teaches and engages with children ages 5 - 12. She has written summer camp curriculum and desires for young people to know who they are in Christ. Holly believes there is no "Junior Jesus" version of the Gospel—children need to know everything about Him that adults know. She firmly advocates that the youngest believers can have the greatest impact on the world!

To learn more:

WWW.HOLLYDUNCAN.COM

Listen my Son